Credit Repair Secrets The Essential Guide to Improving Your Credit Score and Achieving Financial Success

Kiwanis Rucker

This advice contained in this material might not be suitable for everyone. The author designed the information to present her opinion about the subject matter. The reader must carefully investigate all aspects of any decision before committing to him or herself. The author obtained the information contained herein from sources she believes to be reliable and from her own personal experience, but she neither implies not intends any guarantee of accuracy. The author is not in the business of giving legal, accounting, or any other type of professional advice. Should the reader need such advice, he or she must seek services from a competent professional. The author particularly disclaims any liability, loss, or risk taken by individuals who directly or indirectly act on the information contained herein. The author believes the advice presented here is sound, but readers cannot hold her responsible for either the actions they take, or the risk taken by individuals who directly or indirectly act on the information contained herein.

Published by KMJ Publishing House

ISBN: 979-8-218-18424-7

DEDICATION

The book is dedicated to all my sisters and brothers who feel that they are left out of the credit conversations. After today, you will no longer be denied your story.

TABLE OF CONTENTS

ACKNOWLEDGMENTS

To my boys Malik and Jayden, because of you, I push myself every day to be a better person. To my fiancé and my mom, thank you for supporting me no matter how crazy the idea may seem.

CREDIT REPAIR SECRETS TOOLKIT

Before you get started, I want to make sure that I have a place for you to continue your learning. Something that I can update on demand. As you can imagine, updating a book frequently can be challenging, so I have created a **FREE** virtual toolkit that you can access when you scan the QR code.

Inside the toolkit, you will find additional tools, resources, checklist, and bonus content that didn't make it inside the book. If I would have included it all, this book would be twice the size. So, go ahead and scan the QR code for exclusive content. Also, tag me on Instagram **@kiwanisrucker** when you get there.

Remember, this is all about taking action!

CHAPTER ONE
WHO AM I

So, this is going to be super quick, and I promise that I'm going to get right to the point. But it's only right that you know a little background about your favorite credit advisor who wrote this guide and how this credit advisor came to be, so that you can be confident that I can help you get to the credit score that you desire. At 19 years old, I received my first credit card offer in the mail. (I'll never forget, it was an offer from Capital One.) I just had a baby and was working at a hotel restaurant and living in my mom's house. I knew about credit from what I had seen from my mom, but I was never taught about credit and how to use it. So, at 19, with a credit card in one hand and a baby on my hip, I went shopping. Y'all know the rest right…so that card went into collections. I wasn't even responsible enough to make the minimum payments. When I moved from my mom's, I lived in based on income, in a crappy neighborhood because my credit was so bad from one bad credit card that I couldn't get a nice apartment in a nice neighborhood.

Over the next few years, everything I purchased I used cash. My first car was purchased with cash and after it died, I wasn't knowledgeable enough to finance a car from a major car lot. So, my car was purchased at a buy here pay here car company. They say ignorance is bliss and I was truly ignorant about credit. I didn't apply for another credit card until I was 30 years old. (Capital one, they are very forgiving) At the time, I had a 565-credit score simply because the only thing on my credit report were student loans that I wasn't paying. I'm going to fast-forward this a little for y'all. In 2014 I had a 661-credit score. Six credit cards, a new baby (yes, my boys are 16 years apart), and a failed relationship. I was making $32,000 a year and I had $11,000 in credit card debt. So, what did I do? I let them all go into collections. I know, I know, another uninformed decision. However, this time it wasn't one credit card, there were six credit cards and debt collectors were coming after me hard. They weren't trying to help me. Nobody was coming to save me, I had to help myself and that's exactly what I did.

From late 2014 to 2015, I researched all that I could on how to fix my credit and started to put in the work. I worked hard at cleaning up my mess (and not just my credit, but that's a story for another day). I taught myself how to use credit responsibly. My friends and family saw how hard I was working on my credit in 2015 and they began to ask me to help them with their credit, so I did. Helping my family and friends turned into a credit repair company. Which also led to me becoming a Certified Credit Consultant. It is my job to not only help you repair your credit but for you to get an understanding of credit truly and how you can leverage it in your life.

My prayer is that you not just read this guide but that you apply it to your life. Here I stand before you today, having made all the mistakes with my credit but also learned from them, so much so that I have learned to love credit so much that I want to tell the world about it. I want you to learn from my mistakes so that you don't make the same ones that I did. If you have already made some mistakes with your credit, it's ok. I'm here to assist you with cleaning up those mistakes. I believe that everyone deserves a second chance and, in my case, a third chance.

See you on the other side,

Kiwanis Rucker

CHAPTER TWO
GET YOUR MIND RIGHT

Financial success means different things to different people. On a very basic level, financial success means managing your income well enough to take care of your needs. Financial success is not an accident. It doesn't happen overnight. What I challenge you to do is change your mindset about financial success and how you leverage credit to live the life that you say you want to live. You are struggling because you are living with a poverty mindset.

What do I mean by a poverty mindset? It is when you believe your negative self-talk about finances and credit. Many of you are walking around saying, "Well, if it's in God's will,"

Well guess what? It is God's will and you thinking that way is what is keeping you in a poverty mindset. It says in the Bible that He came to give you life and give it to you abundantly. Also, there are some of you who are in a poverty mindset because your actions do not back up the lifestyle that you say you want to live. I want it to be clear, you can make all the money in the world and still have a poverty mindset.

What I want to challenge you to do is to break

that poverty mindset. Now I do want you to give yourself a little grace because breaking the poverty mindset is not going to happen overnight. Many of us were born into a poverty mindset. It is in our bloodline. What you think about credit today is shaped by the way that you were brought up and all your life experiences. You probably heard negative messages about credit when you were growing up. So, it's not surprising that issues of credit can cause strong emotions.

One of the ways that you can break the poverty mindset is by doing things differently, not just thinking differently about credit and finances but by also doing differently. For some of you, this may mean creating a spending plan. For others, this may mean talking about those negative emotions that come up when you are not at your best, which causes you to make poor decisions with your money and credit.

I've heard people talk about how cash is king or that they don't need credit. I've even heard people say that they will just wait seven years for things to fall off their credit report. Contrary to popular belief, you need credit. Credit controls a lot of things around us. Your credit will determine if you can get a car, rent an apartment, open a bank account, pay a deposit on utilities, and even determine your car insurance rates. I can’t stress how important credit is and why you should take it seriously.

I’m sure you can tell by now that a lot of this credit stuff is related to what's happening in the mind. Mindset is everything. Because without the right mindset, you're not going to give yourself the energy that you need to succeed. So, I challenge you friend, as you are working on your credit, also do the inner work to change the way that you not only think but also act.

NOTES

CHAPTER THREE
WHAT CREDIT REALLY IS

I don't want to bore you, but I do want you to be informed so that these creditors and credit bureaus can't try you. So, let's start by talking about what credit is. Credit is a financial arrangement in which a lender extends a loan to a borrower, with the understanding that the loan will be repaid later, typically with interest. Credit can take many forms, including credit cards, mortgages, personal loans, and business loans.

One of the main purposes of credit is to allow individuals and businesses to borrow money to make purchases or investments that they may not have the funds for upfront. This can be especially useful for large purchases, such as buying a home, car, or starting a business, which may require a significant amount of money that an individual or company may not have on hand.

Credit is typically extended by financial institutions, such as banks, credit unions, and online lenders, as well as by non-financial institutions, such as retailers and car dealerships. These lenders assess an applicant's creditworthiness before deciding whether to extend credit and the terms of the loan, such as the interest rate and repayment period, are typically based on the borrower's credit score and financial history.

A credit score is a numerical representation of an individual's creditworthiness based on their credit history and other financial factors. Credit scores are typically used by lenders to determine the risk of lending to a borrower, with higher scores indicating a lower risk of default. Credit scores are typically calculated using information from credit reports, which are generated by credit bureaus and contain details about an individual's credit history, including information about their credit accounts, payment history, and outstanding balances.

Besides credit scores, lenders also consider other factors when deciding whether to extend credit, such as an applicant's income, employment history, and debt-to-income ratio. The debt-to-income ratio is a measure of an individual's financial stability and is calculated by dividing their monthly debt payments by their monthly gross income. A high debt-to-income ratio may indicate that an individual is overextended and may have difficulty repaying their debts.

There are several different types of credit that individuals and businesses can apply for. These are just a few:

Credit cards: Credit cards are perhaps the most common form of credit. They allow individuals to borrow money on a short-term basis to make purchases or withdraw cash. Credit cards typically have a credit limit, which is the maximum amount that can be borrowed at any given time, and an interest rate, which is the percentage of the borrowed amount that must be paid back plus the principal. Credit card interest rates are typically variable, meaning that they can fluctuate based on market conditions.

Mortgages: A mortgage is a type of loan that is used to purchase a home. Mortgages are typically secured by the home itself, meaning that if the borrower defaults on the loan, the lender can foreclose on the property and sell it to recoup their losses. Mortgages are typically offered by banks and other financial institutions, and the terms of the loan, such as the interest rate and repayment period, are typically based on the borrower's credit score and financial history.

Personal loans: Personal loans are unsecured loans that can be used for a variety of purposes, such as consolidating debt, paying medical bills, or financing a home renovation. Personal loans are typically offered by banks and other financial institutions, and the terms of the loan are typically based on the borrower's credit score and financial history.

Car loans: A car loan is a type of loan that is used specifically to finance the purchase of a new or used vehicle. It is typically offered by banks, credit unions, and other financial institutions and allows the borrower to pay for a car over a specified period, usually several years, with regular monthly payments. The amount of the loan, interest rate, and repayment period are determined based on the borrower's credit score and financial situation. A car loan typically requires collateral in the form of the vehicle being purchased, and the lender may have the right to seize the vehicle if the borrower fails to make their payments.

NOTES

CHAPTER FOUR
HOW CREDIT SCORES ARE CACULATED

I don't want to spend a lot of time here because I believe that credit scores are vanity metrics. They are like someone who is obsessed with how many likes the picture of their dog gets on social media. If you make corrections to your credit report, the credit score will reflect this. However, I do want you to understand how your score is calculated.

Your credit score is 100% and is broken down into 35% payment history, 30% the amount that you owe, 15% the length of your credit history. 10% credit mix and 10% new credit.

Let's break these down some more. Payment history is 35% of your credit score. Before lending you money, the lender wants to know that you can pay them back. They want to look at what you've done in the past to make sure that you've paid other lenders back on time.

Then you have the amount owed, which is 30% of your credit score. If you're using a lot of your available credit, this is an indication to a lender that you may be overextended.

We have 15%, which is the length of your credit history, and that's just what it is. How long have you had credit? Is your credit established?

10% is your credit mix. How many kinds of credit accounts do you have on your credit report? Having different kinds of credit accounts helps to show that you can manage different types of credit.

Last is 10% of new credit. Those are your credit inquiries. So how many lines of credit do you have, and how much are you applying for new credit? Opening too many credit accounts in a short amount of time can be seen as a risk to lenders. You don't want to make it seem like you're doing a lot of credit card shopping.

Let's talk a little about the shop around rule. In circumstances where you want to shop around to get the best terms and interest rates, FICO understands that and it allows you to shop around for home loans, auto loans, and student loans. Now you must keep these types of inquiries within a 30-day timeframe, and they will count as one inquiry versus multiple inquiries. One inquiry can lower your credit score by 1-5 points. Ensure that the companies that you're shopping around with list the type of inquiry correctly.

Here is a chart of FICO score ranges:
FICO Score ranges from 300-850
781 or higher = Excellent
661-780= Good
601-660 = Fair
500-600 = Poor
300-499 = Very Poor

NOTES

CHAPTER FIVE
CONSUMER LAWS

Consumer laws are laws that protect consumers who borrow money or use credit in their financial transactions. These laws set standards for the practices of lenders and creditors and provide consumers with certain rights when it comes to borrowing money or using credit. Some examples of credit consumer laws include the Truth in Lending Act, the Fair Credit Reporting Act, and the Fair Debt Collection Practices Act. These laws regulate various aspects of the credit and lending industry, such as the disclosure of interest rates and fees, the accuracy of credit reports, and the behavior of debt collectors. Let's dive a bit into the three main consumer laws that you should know about.

The Truth in Lending Act (TILA): is a federal law that requires lenders to disclose the terms and conditions of consumer credit to borrowers. The law was passed in 1968 to protect consumers from deceptive lending practices and to promote informed decision-making about credit. Under TILA, lenders are required to disclose certain information to borrowers, including the annual percentage rate (APR), finance charges, and the total number of payments. This information must be provided in a clear and concise manner, using standardized forms and language. The purpose of these disclosures is to help borrowers compare the costs and terms of different credit offers and to understand the terms of the credit they are being offered.

TILA also includes requirements that protect consumers from certain types of credit practices that are considered deceptive or unfair. For example, it prohibits lenders from charging unexpected or hidden fees and from making false or misleading statements about credit terms. It also gives consumers the right to cancel certain types of credit transactions within a certain period of time. TILA is enforced by the Consumer Financial Protection Bureau (CFPB) and private consumers can bring lawsuits against lenders or other parties who violate the law.

The Fair Credit Reporting Act (FCRA): is a federal law in the United States that regulates the collection, distribution, and use of consumer credit information. It was passed in 1970 to promote the correctness, fairness, and privacy of consumer credit information and to provide consumers with the right to dispute errors on their credit reports.

The FCRA has several key requirements that affect consumer credit reporting. For example, it requires credit reporting agencies (CRAs) to maintain reasonable procedures to ensure the correctness of credit reports and to investigate disputes that consumers raise about errors on their credit reports. It also requires CRAs to provide consumers with a copy of their credit report upon request and to provide a summary of their rights under the FCRA. In addition, the FCRA limits the information that CRAs can include in credit reports and sets forth requirements for the use of credit reports by lenders and other users.

The FCRA is enforced by the Consumer Financial Protection Bureau (CFPB) and private consumers can bring lawsuits against credit reporting agencies or others who violate the law.

The Fair Debt Collection Practices Act (FDCPA): is a federal law that controls the actions of debt collectors when they try to collect debts from consumers. The law was passed in 1978 to protect consumers from abusive, deceptive, and unfair debt collection practices.

Under the FDCPA, debt collectors are prohibited from using abusive or threatening language, making false or misleading statements, and engaging in other deceptive practices when collecting debts. They are also required to respect consumers' rights to privacy and to provide certain information about the debt, such as the amount of the debt and the creditor, to the consumer when requested. The FDCPA applies to debt collectors who are collecting debts on behalf of someone else, such as a credit card company or a creditor. It does not apply to friends and family collecting their own debts. The FDCPA is enforced by the Consumer Financial Protection Bureau (CFPB) and private consumers can bring lawsuits against debt collectors or other parties who violate the law.

NOTES

CHAPTER SIX
THE BIG THREE

There are a lot of credit bureaus, however the three that you should focus on are Experian, Equifax, and TransUnion. These are the credit bureaus that are widely used.

Experian

Experian also offers other financial products and services, such as identity theft protection and credit monitoring. The company collects and maintains financial information on individuals and businesses, which is used to generate credit reports and credit scores.

Equifax

Like Experian, Equifax offers a wide range of products and services, one of them being collecting and maintaining information that generates your credit report and score. Equifax is based in Atlanta, GA. In 2017, Equifax announced a data breach that exposed the personal information of 143 million people.

TransUnion

TransUnion rounds out the big three. Just like Experian and Equifax, TransUnion collects information to generate your credit report and score.

CREDIT BUREAUS CONTACT INFORMATION

Experian:
Address: P.O. Box 9701 Allen, TX 75013
Phone Number: 1.888.397.3742
Fax: 973.390.3838
Website: www.Experian.com

Equifax
Address: P.O. Box 740241 Atlanta, GA 30374
Phone Number: 1.800.685.1111
Fax: 1.888.826.0549
Website: www.Equifax.com

TransUnion
P.O. Box 2000
Chester, PA 19016
1.800.916.8800
Fax: 1.888.462.8009
www.Transunion.com

NOTES

CHAPTER SEVEN
WHERE TO GET YOUR CREDIT REPORT

Now that you understand what credit is, how credit scores are calculated, and know your rights, let's get to work.

Here are the steps you can follow to get your credit report:

1. Determine which credit reporting agency(s) you want to request a report from. You have the right to a free copy of your credit report from each of the three major credit reporting agencies once every 12 months. You can request your reports from all three agencies at the same time, or you can request them separately.

2. Go to the Annual Credit Report website (www.annualcreditreport.com). This is the only website that is authorized by the federal government to provide free credit reports. Do not use any other website that claims to offer free credit reports, as many of these websites are scams and may try to sell you credit-related products or services.

3. Click on the "Request your free credit

reports" button. You will be taken to a page where you can select which credit reporting agencies you want to request reports from. You can choose to request all three reports at the same time, or you can request them separately.

4. Follow the prompts to provide your personal information. You will be asked to provide your name, address, date of birth, and social security number. You may also be asked to provide additional personal information, such as your employment history or current salary.

5. Verify your identity. The credit reporting agencies will ask you to provide information that only you would know, such as the name of your current or previous employer, the amount of your current mortgage or rent payment, or the name of your bank. This is to ensure that only you can access your credit report.

6. In most cases, you will have access to your credit report immediately. However, there may be some cases where you will have to wait for your

credit report to be mailed to you.

Now there are other places where you can get a copy of your credit report. Most of the credit monitoring services are going to come with a cost. I do not suggest using Credit Karma. My suggestion is that if you are serious about repairing your credit (which I hope that you are), you should use a credit monitoring services. I say this because you will have access to all three major credit reports once per month, you will have access to your credit score once per month, and most credit monitoring services will have identity theft monitoring.

Be aware of impostors. There are a lot of websites that will offer you a free credit report. Many times, there will be strings attached. Be aware of these. The only place to get a free credit report is annualcreditreport.com. Also, annualcreditreport.com will verify your personal information on the site. You should not be redirected to another site or receive anything in your email.

NOTES

CHAPTER EIGHT
HOW TO READ YOUR CREDIT REPORT

Once you get a copy of your credit report, it's important to know how to read it. There are going to be numbers, abbreviations, and terms you've never seen before. Don't worry, I'm going to walk you through this.

A credit report is divided into four sections: identifying information, credit history, public records, and inquiries. Identifying information is just that, information that identifies you. Look at it closely to make sure it's all correct. It's not unusual for there to be two or three spellings of your name, more than one Social Security number, or a few addresses (if you move around a lot). That's usually because someone reported the information that way. You want to make sure that everything is corrected. You should only have one name, one Social Security number, one current address, and one employer if it is reported. While correcting this information will not increase your credit score, it will make you look good to creditors.

On most credit reports, the public records section will be located near the top of the credit report. In this section, you will find any judgments, bankruptcies, tax liens, garnishments, or foreclosures that you may have. If you do not have these, this section will be blank.

The next section is your credit history. Sometimes, the individual accounts are called trade lines. Each account will include the name of the creditor, and the account number, which may show with a few numbers in the beginning and then multiple "X'.

The accounts will also include:

- When you opened the account
- The kind of credit (installment, such as a mortgage or car loan, or revolving, such as a department store credit card)
- Whether the account is in your name alone or with another person (joint).
- The total amount of the loan, high credit limit or highest balance of the account.
- How much do you still owe.
- Fixed monthly payments or minimum monthly amount.
- Status of the account (open, inactive, closed, paid, charge-off).
- How well you've paid the account over the last two years.

Credit accounts are divided into five categories: real estate, installment, revolving, collection and other.

Here is a better description of each category:

- Real Estate: First and second mortgage loans on your home.
- Installment: Accounts comprised of fixed terms with regular payments, such as a car loan.
- Revolving: Accounts with opened terms with varying payments, such as a credit card account.
- Collection: Accounts seriously past due that have been assigned to an attorney or collection agency.
- Other: Accounts where the exact category is unknown. This could include 30-day accounts, such as an American Express card.

You want to review this section of the credit report carefully. You should look for any mistakes within the accounts like incorrect balances, incorrect status, accounts that do not belong to you, accounts that show the incorrect type, or if an account is reporting a missed payment that was never missed. It is your right to have a credit report that is 100% correct and accurate at all times. 79% of all credit reports have errors, so it's more likely than not that you will find errors on your credit report too.

TIP: Most collection accounts report inaccurately. This is grounds for disputing. We will talk about collection accounts later.

The next section of your credit report is the inquiry section. This section will show you exactly who has reviewed your credit report over the last two years.

There are three types of inquiries. There are soft inquiries; these are when a company you've already done business with pulls your credit report or when you yourself pull your credit report from websites like Credit Karma. Soft inquiries have no negative impact on your credit score.

You also have promotional inquiries. These types of inquiries happen when the credit bureaus sell your data to different companies who are looking for consumers to market their products to. Normally you must fit into a certain condition for this to happen. Most of these are going to be from those credit card offers you get in the mail. These kinds of inquiries also have no impact on your credit score.

The third type of inquiry is your hard inquiry, and this is where you have given your written permission to a creditor to pull your credit report when you have completed an application for a loan or a credit card. These inquiries are the inquiries that affect your credit score. Remember, they can lower your credit score by 1-5 points per inquiry.

The last part of your credit report will be a list of all your creditors and their contact information.

Your Equifax report uses payment codes ranging from 1 to 9; and R1 or I1 are codes that show how well your payment history is. Often, the code key will be listed on the report so you can better understand what the codes mean.

NOTES

CHAPTER NINE
COMMONT CREDIT REPORT ERRORS

As I stated in the previous chapter, 79% of Americans have errors in their credit report. Remember that the information provided to the credit bureaus comes from the company providing the credit. The credit bureaus do not double-check this information.

Here is a list of some of the most common credit report errors:

- Incorrect names, phone numbers, addresses, social security number
- An account that belongs to Sr. but is reported as Jr.
- Duplicate accounts
- Wrong credit limits
- Incorrect activity dates
- Past due payments that are not past due
- Public records that don't belong to you
- Accounts that don't belong to you
- Outdated information
- Incorrect account status
- Closed account that was reported as open
- Ex-spouse listed on your credit report
- Incorrect account number

- Charge-off reporting a balance
- Inquiries you didn't authorize
- Paid accounts that are still reflecting a balance
- Payment terms
- Incorrect high balance
- Incorrect date of last activity

NOTES

CHAPTER TEN

CREATING A CREDIT REPAIR PLAN

Before you start disputing errors on your credit report, you want to create a plan for repairing your credit. Everything you do with your credit from here on out will be strategic.

You will now gather all the errors that you have found within your credit report. The best way to do this is by creating a spreadsheet of all the errors that you found, the account you found them on, and the credit bureau that is reporting the error. This will be your credit repair plan. At this point you will also want to gather any supporting documents that you have that support your disputes.

I also want to be real with you here repairing your credit is not an overnight process it will take some time. Just think if this was easy everyone would have excellent credit scores. Around 48 million Americans have a credit score between 300-579, which is considered a poor credit score.

Now with this information in hand, you will start the dispute process which we will talk about next.

NOTES

CHAPTER ELEVN

UNDERSTANDING THE DISPUTE PROCESS

What is a dispute letter? I'm glad you asked. Simply put, a dispute letter is a letter that you write to the credit bureaus, the original creditors, or any collection agencies saying that you do not agree with what they are reporting on your credit report. In your dispute letter, there will be an explanation of an error or outdated information on your credit report that you want to be corrected. You'll want to dispute the account with the bureau that is reporting the incorrect information. You may find that an account is on one credit report that may not be on the other two reports. Or you may see an account on two credit reports that may not be on the third report. You may even have some accounts that are not reported to the credit bureaus at all.

Let me dig a little deeper into that. Companies must pay credit bureaus to report on your credit report. Not every company is going to pay every bureau to report on your credit report.

An example: TransUnion is reporting an account, but the account is not reporting on your Equifax and Experian credit reports. This is because the company that is giving TransUnion the information is only paying for the account to report with TransUnion. You want to make sure that when you're reviewing your credit report and you're writing your disputes, you are sending your letters to the correct place. The items that you should dispute are all of the items that you listed as errors or inaccurate when you were creating your credit repair plan.

Any incorrect, inaccurate information can be disputed. I don't care what it may be, even if it's student loans. If you have an account on your credit report and there maybe be a slight error, but the account is helping your report more than it's hurting your report, you don't want to have that account deleted. It will more than likely hurt your score more than help it if you have it deleted. In this case, you should just have this account updated with the correct information. Remember, credit scores consider all payment history, past and present.

So, if you see an error in your account, review it thoroughly to see if there is more positive payment history than negative. Remember what I said, everything you do with your credit must be strategic.
Let's talk about how to write an effective

dispute letter. When you're writing your dispute letters, you never use dispute letters online. I know I've talked about this a million times. The credit bureaus receive thousands of these generic letters every day. Not only that, these letters make you look like a joke to the credit bureaus, and they will not take you seriously. You want them to know that you are serious about your credit. So instead of using a draft of a letter that you Googled, you want to write a letter in your own words. In your letter, you will simply let the credit bureaus know exactly what it is you want them to do. Do you want it removed? If so, say that. Do you want it updated with the correct information? If so, say that. You don't need to sound like a lawyer reciting credit laws or a credit guru. You want to sound like a real person because you are. I have provided you with some templates at the end of this book that you can take and write in your own words.

Let's talk about what you should dispute first. You should always dispute personal information first and in a separate letter from your other disputes. I say this because those disputes are usually resolved very easily and quickly, usually within 15 days. Once you receive those updates back from the credit bureaus, you should dispute any account information. Now you can use one letter to dispute multiple accounts. The credit bureaus have 30-45 days to investigate your dispute.

If you are disputing collection accounts, you want to dispute with the collection agency and the credit bureau at the same time. Now I would dispute collection accounts separate from, say, charge-offs. Make sure that you tell the credit bureaus exactly what you want to happen. You always want to have a collection account removed from your credit report.

CREDIT REPAIR DISPUTE PROCESS

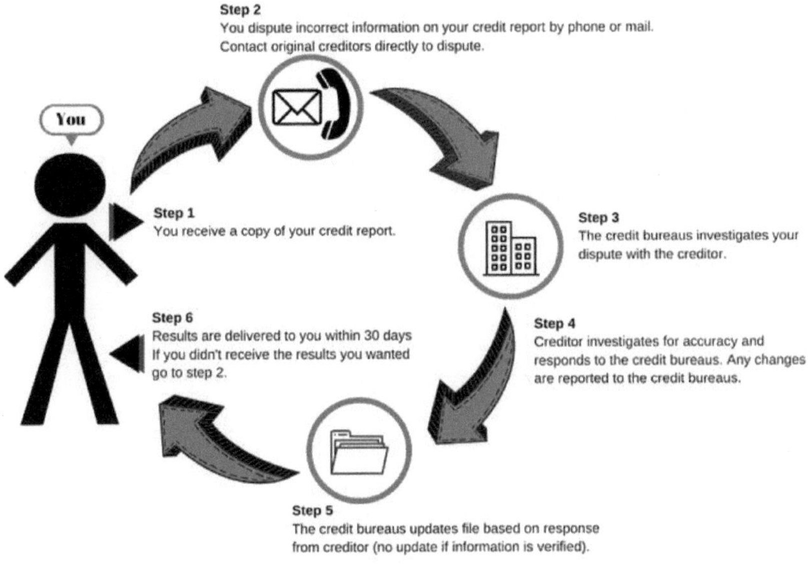

You

Step 1
You receive a copy of your credit report.

Step 2
You dispute incorrect information on your credit report by phone or mail. Contact original creditors directly to dispute.

Step 3
The credit bureaus investigates your dispute with the creditor.

Step 4
Creditor investigates for accuracy and responds to the credit bureaus. Any changes are reported to the credit bureaus.

Step 5
The credit bureaus updates file based on response from creditor (no update if information is verified).

Step 6
Results are delivered to you within 30 days
If you didn't receive the results you wanted go to step 2.

NOTES

CHAPTER TWELVE
HOW TO HANDLE DEBT COLLECTORS

Aside from a public record, collections are one of the most damaging negative items on your credit report. They can really lower your credit score.

There are two types of collectors. Those who have been assigned the debt and those who have purchased the debt. For collectors that have been assigned the debt, I would consult with the original creditor directly. This allows you to make payment arrangements directly with the original creditor whom you have the contract with.

My advice when handling collections is to know your rights. Collection agencies will call you and send you letters in the mail. Make sure that you are opening all your mail.

For collectors that have purchased the debt, the collection agency must show you that you owe them in accordance with the law, they have to show that they have the right to collect on that debt. They must show proof that you have done business with them. Make them show you that they have a contract signed by you. Request that they show proof that you owe them. Understand that proof is not the last bill. You want something that shows that you are bound to that debt with them in accordance with the law. There's no law that states that you must do business with that debt collector. You can simply write a letter to that collection agency and state that, hey, I am not doing business with you. If you ignore them, they can report the debt on your credit report. They can also try to file a lawsuit to get you to pay them.

So how does a collection agency purchase debt? Let's dig into that some. Collection agencies typically purchase debt in bulk from original creditors, such as credit card companies, banks, or hospitals, at a discounted price. The agencies then attempt to collect the full amount owed from the consumer. The original creditor may sell the debt if they are unable to collect on it and see it as a loss, or if they want to free up resources to focus on other debts. The collection agency earns a profit by collecting more than what they paid for the debt.

For example, ABC collection agency contacts T-Mobile and asks them if they can purchase accounts that are past due 100 days that owe about $400. They will purchase these accounts for $4 dollars. They will then try to collect the

$400. Now, remember T-Mobile has already written the account off in their books.

Before you contact a collection agency, either in writing or over the phone, you want to make sure that you know your state's statute of limitations. Now, what's next? What if they can prove that you owe them the debt they are trying to collect on? 9 times out of 10 times they can't but what if it does happen? I am not telling you not to pay your debts. You should pay your debts, but you always want to pay them to the original creditor. What I'm going to suggest is that if this happens, you can negotiate with the collection agency to pay the debt, but you will always want to negotiate a pay for delete.

A pay for delete is if you make the payment, they will delete the collection account from your credit report. I want you to understand that a pay for delete is against the collection agency agreement with the credit bureaus. This doesn't mean that they don't do it. If you can't negotiate a pay for delete, I would pursue trying to get the collection off your credit report based on the inaccuracies.

So how can you handle a collection call? If a

collection agency contacts you, don't avoid the call. Just answer the call. **DO NOT VERIFY ANY INFORMATION.**

So, the call may go a little like this:

Company: Hello this is a call from ABC company. This is an attempt to collect a debt. My name is Kathy. May I speak to Kiwanis?

You: This is Kiwanis.

Company: Will you please verify the last four digits of your social security number?

This is where you should end the call by saying please only contact me through the address you have on file and simply hang up.

After you have received a collection call, you can write the company a cease-and-desist letter. You can go online and look up the address of the collection company. In your letter, you can tell the company that you are disputing the validity of the claim that you do not owe them anything and for them to only contact you through the mail.

NOTES

CHAPTER THIRTEEN
THE ANATOMY OF A DUNNING LETTER

When you receive a collection letter in the mail, they will say that it is an attempt to collect a debt. This is a dunning letter. Don't ignore this letter. The letter should show the amount they are trying to collect, the original creditor, and one of the most important parts is the letter will let you know you have the right to dispute the debt they are trying to collect. Sometimes the letter will be sent before the account is reported to the credit bureaus. You do not want to ignore them.

When you receive a dunning letter, you want to contact the collection agency in writing as soon as possible. The letter that you will send is called debt validation. Debt validation is a process by which a creditor or debt collection agency must provide proof that a debt is legitimate. During the debt validation process, the collection agency must provide documentation such as the original loan agreement, payment history, and any other relevant information to prove that the debt is valid. If the collection agency is unable to provide adequate proof that the debt is legitimate, you are not required to pay the debt. Check out the templates for an example of a debt validation letter.

DUNNING LETTER EXAMPLE

PO Box 528
Goodlettsville TN 37070-0528
ADDRESS SERVICE REQUESTED

FOX
COLLECTION CENTER

615-559-4015
888-633-0384

454 Moss Trail ♦ Goodlettsville TN 37072

January 18, 2023

Pay on line at www.payfoxcollection.com

Fox Account #	**Creditor Account #**
PIN #	**Amount Due** $113.82

DEMAND FOR PAYMENT OF DEBT

This is a second demand for payment in full of the accounts listed below.

Payment in full should be sent to the address below, or you may pay online. You may call our office at (615) 559-4015 or 888-633-0384 to speak with an account representative about these accounts.

Creditor	**Creditor Account #**	**Amount Due**
		$ 113.82

AMOUNT DUE: $ 113.82

This communication is an attempt to collect a debt by a debt collector. Any information obtained will be used for that purpose.

This collection agency is licensed by the Collection Service Board of the Tennessee Department of Commerce and Insurance.

---Detach and Return with Payment---

Pay on line at www.payfoxcollection.com
Or pay by MasterCard, Visa, Discover or check.
Checks may be processed electronically.

Please charge to my: ☐  ☐  ☐  ☐ HSA

Fox Account #	**Creditor Account #**
PIN #	**Amount Due** $113.82

Card Number: ____________________________

Expiration Date ______/______

Security Code (from back of card) ______________

Payment Amount: $ ________________________

Signature ______________________________

FOX COLLECTION CENTER
PO Box 528
Goodlettsville TN 37070-0528

NOTES

CHAPTER FOURTEEN
JUDGEMENTS, BANKRUPTCY, TAX LIENS, OH MY!

Any public record on your credit report will have a huge impact on your credit report, just like collection accounts. One of the good things about these kinds of accounts is the older they get, the less impact they have on your credit score. A bankruptcy or a tax lien that is five years old will not have as big of an impact on your credit as, say, a bankruptcy or tax lien that is one year old. However, we still want to address these accounts when we are repairing our credit.

While other accounts on your credit report are supplied voluntarily by the creditor, public records are not. The credit bureaus hire third-party vendors to look up public record information and submit that information to the credit bureaus for it to be reported on your credit report. You read it right, there are actually people that go to the courthouse and they look up this information. They look for everything, judgments, tax liens, and bankruptcies.

Here is what you can do to tackle public records:

- Review your credit report for any errors within the public record (make sure to look for dates, the name of the courthouse, the responsible person, the attorney's name, status, and where you served properly). You want to make sure everything is 100% accurate and complete.

- If everything is accurate and complete, you should challenge the public record with the courthouse or if it's a tax lien, you want to do that with the IRS (remember you have the right to have a credit report that is 100% verifiable).

- Compare the paperwork that you have to the information that's on the credit report. Is it 100% accurate and complete? If not, it needs to be corrected or removed.

- Go after the account. Look to see if the public record itself is valid (look for misspelled names, incorrect accounts number, is the original creditor correct, your address, was the balance collected, is the balance correct).

- Once a public record is formally

challenged, it is now the responsibility of the creditor to prove that the public record is correct. This is also true with tax liens. I will never tell you not to pay your debts, so remember removing the public record will not get rid of the debt.

Now that we have talked a little about judgments and tax liens, let's talk a little about bankruptcies because they are going to be a little different.

When you're looking at a bankruptcy on your credit report, you want to make sure that you look at the actual accounts that were discharged within that bankruptcy before you go after the actual bankruptcy itself. You want to again make sure that all the account information is 100% accurate and correct. Any errors within the account, you want to dispute the account using a dispute letter that we talked about earlier. You want to remove those accounts from your credit report first. Once the accounts have been removed, you then want to dispute the actual bankruptcy. You can dispute the actual bankruptcy with the courthouse. What you are going to receive from the courthouse will be something saying that they don't report to credit bureaus, which remember, I told you the credit bureaus pay people to go looking for public records, so this is true. You will then make a copy of what you received from the courthouse and send it to the credit bureaus and ask to have the bankruptcy removed from your credit report.

One of the most asked questions is about child support, so let's dig a little into that. Now I only want you to do this if you are current on your payments. If not, the late payments will continue to report on your credit report.

If you have child support that is reported on your credit report. You can write to the courthouse wherever the child support is and dispute the information with that courthouse. Again, you should get something returned from the courthouse saying they don't report to the credit bureaus. You want to send a copy of this information to the credit bureaus and ask them to remove it.

NOTES

CHAPTER FIFTEEN
CHARGE-OFFS AND PAST DUE PAYMENTS

Let's move on to talk about charge-offs and what they are and how to address past due payments.

Simply put a charge-off is an entry on your credit report that indicates a creditor, after trying to get you to pay, they have given up and they closed the account.

Charge-offs hurt your credit report just as much as collection accounts and public records. They will affect your ability to borrow money and lower your credit score. I will say it again just because the creditor has given up trying to collect, you still owe the debt. Also, remember that these charged-off accounts are sold or assigned to collection agencies. The best way to avoid a charge-off account is to try to work with the creditor if you can't make your payments. Often creditors have programs that help you make your payments.

Like any other account on your credit report, the best way to pursue a deletion or an update is to find something that is incorrect within the account.

Tip: If the charge-off is showing a credit

limit, that is incorrect, the charge-off should not show a credit limit.

Remember that we talked about being strategic, the older the charge-off gets, the less effect it has on your credit report. You want to look at the charge off carefully. Make sure you aren't having something removed that may be helping you.

If you miss the payment on one of your bills, the late payment can get reported to the credit bureaus once you're at least 30 days past the due date.

However, penalties and or fees could kick in even if you're only one day late. If you bring your account current before the 30-day mark, the late payment may not be reported to the credit bureaus. Make sure you work with your creditors before missing your payment.

Late payments that are newer can decrease your credit score. However, as they age, they have less of an effect on your credit score as well.

If you have one or two lay payments, you can send a goodwill letter to the creditor and ask them if they will remove the late payment out of good faith. All they can do is say yes or no. It never hurts to try to send that goodwill letter. Now only do this if you have a good payment history and only were only truly late on one or two payments.

NOTES

CHAPTER SIXTEEN
FILING A COMPLAINT

If an account has come back verified a couple of times you want to request the credit bureau's method of verification.

According to section 611 of the Fair Credit Reporting Act, upon request, the bureau must provide a consumer with a description of how the investigation was conducted no later than 15 days after receipt.

You can request to see information on the account's accuracy within your credit report, and this is per section 609 of the Fair Credit Reporting Act.

You should also be disputing directly with the original creditor. In section 623 of the Fair Credit Reporting Act, it puts as much of the responsibility for accurate and complete reporting on the company that is providing the information as it does on the credit bureaus.

When all else fails you've been persistent, you stayed on it, it's come back verified over and over again. You can go and now file a complaint with the Attorney General and with the Consumer Financial Protection Bureau.

Each state has a Consumer Protection Audit office that will assist you with speaking to the original creditors directly to resolve your dispute. Most creditors do not want to deal with the Attorney General and the Consumer Financial Protection Bureaus so they will try to resolve your issue as soon as possible.

If the credit bureaus, original creditors, or collection agency fail to report accurate and verifiable information on your credit report. This is against your rights, and you should file a complaint to assist you with enforcing compliance only if you have done all the things first.

So how do you file that complaint? The website to file the complaint with the consumer finance agency is consumer finance.gov/complaint.

You can file that complaint with the Attorney General's office that is in your state. You can look up your state's website to look up that contact information.

You will need to include in your complaint any key facts in your own words. Being organized will come in handy here. You need to have dates, amounts, and any communications you've had with the credit bureaus and the original creditors. You want to include that in your complaint documentation. You also want to include any letters that have come back from the credit bureaus and the original creditors. You do have a 50-page limit, so again, be organized, straight to the point, and as detailed as possible.

NOTES

CHAPTER SEVENTEEN
BUSTING THE MYTHS

There are a lot of so-called “credit gurus” out there who are spreading a lot of misinformation. It’s my job to make sure that you have the correct information. So, we are going to bust some of those myths that you have heard for years.

"Paying off old debts will instantly improve my credit score."

Now I would never tell you not to pay your debts. However, paying old debts will not improve your credit score.

"I can remove accurate negative information from my credit report."

It is your right to have a credit report that is 100% accurate. However, if the negative information on your credit report is accurate, you can’t have it removed.

"Closing credit accounts will help my credit score."

Closing a credit account will not help your credit score. In fact, it may hurt your score more than help it. Be sure before you close an account that you are reviewing that account thoroughly. But don’t despair if you close an account, your score will decrease some but should rebound.

"I can fix my credit by hiring a credit repair company."

You can fix your credit by hiring a credit repair company, but you can also do it yourself if you have the time, patience, and know-how.

"I can just ignore my bad credit and it will go away."

It will not just go away. Just think, while you are waiting seven years for things to fall off your credit report, you are missing out on a lot of opportunities and paying more for the things that you want and need.

"All credit scores are the same."

All credit scores are not created equal. Everyone's situation is different. What may be one person's credit score may not be yours.

"I need to have a perfect credit score to get approved for credit."

You don't need a perfect credit score to get approved for credit. However, being in the best possible position with your credit score when you need it is helpful.

"I can use a new Social Security Number to start a new credit history."

No, No, No, and No. This is against the law. You can't use a new Social Security Number to start a new credit history.

"Once you ruin your credit, you'll never rebuild it."

This is simply not true. While it will take some work on your part as well as some time, you can eventually rebuild your credit.

"Checking my own credit report will hurt my credit score."

Checking your credit score will not lower your credit score. You can check your credit report as often as you like. So go ahead and get to checking.

"If your dispute comes back verified, then that is just what it is."

Don't let these credit bureaus play with you. Nine times out of ten, they didn't do what they were supposed to do. Don't give up sending another dispute and demand the credit bureaus do their job. Keep going until you get the results that you are looking for.

NOTES

CHAPTER EIGHTEEN
ESTABLISHING NEW CREDIT

It's important that when you are establishing credit or re-establishing credit not to go out and start applying for just anything. You don't want your score to decrease because of too many inquiries. You can always call any company that you are thinking about applying to and ask them about their qualifications. If you meet those qualifications, go for it. This is what I recommend.

Piggybacking: Piggybacking is when you ask someone that you trust to add you as an authorized user to their oldest credit card with the highest limit. You also want to ensure that the credit card company will report authorized users to the credit bureaus. I can't stress enough here that this should be someone you trust. You want to make sure they are paying their bills and paying on time. Whatever they are doing with that credit card will be reported on your credit report too. The point of this is to get their good credit history added to your credit report to help increase your credit score.

Secured Credit Card: A secured credit card is an excellent way to help increase your credit score. You make a cash deposit, normally it's between $300 and $500. Whatever your cash deposit is, that is going to be your credit limit. If you show good usage over time, the credit card company may give you back that cash deposit, convert the credit card to an unsecured credit card, and increase your credit limit. You only need one secured credit card. My favorite one that I always recommend is the Discover Card.

Credit Union: A credit union is good for those who don't have credit or have very little credit.

Credit Builder Loans: A credit builder loan works differently than a traditional loan. The credit builder holds the amount borrowed in an account while you make payments. So, for example, say you borrow $1,000. The company would hold the $1,000 in the account while you make small payments monthly on the $1,000. Once you reach the $1,000, you will be sent a check for that amount. You are increasing your credit because they report your payments monthly to the credit bureaus while saving. The company that I recommend is Self Credit Builder.

Fintech Companies: Fintech credit cards are credit cards issued by financial technology (fintech) companies rather than traditional banks or financial institutions. These companies use technology to provide a more convenient, user-friendly, and personalized experience for consumers and may offer features such as cashback rewards, budgeting tools, and real-time transaction alerts. Some fintech credit cards may also be designed for specific groups of consumers, such as students or small business owners. An example of a Fintech Card is Tomo Credit. With Tomo Credit, they will link to your bank account to determine your credit limit rather than using your credit report. To be approved for their credit card, you must have a minimum of $800 in the bank accounts that you link. You can link more than one account to get approved. Now beware, there are also some other requirements with these companies, like making weekly payments and automatic payments.

Local Finance Companies: This is my least favorite way to start building credit, however it is helpful. These loans normally have higher interest rates. Make sure that if you choose to use a finance company, you choose a company that reports to the credit bureaus. I would also recommend doing your research on the company before doing business with them. There are some horror stories out there about finance companies.

NOTES

CHAPTER NINETEEN
WHAT'S NEXT

Now that you have done all the things and you have repaired your credit. What's next? I have eight tips for you along the way.

The number one tip that I have is to pay everything on time. Payment history accounts for 35% of your score. This is weighed very heavily, so paying everything on time can have a huge impact on increasing your scores in the short and long term.

The second tip is to keep your credit card balances low. Utilization accounts for 30% of your score. So, you want to make sure you know the limits on all your cards. You don't want to let any balance on your card go over 10% of that limit. So, for example, if you have a credit card limit on one of your cards, that's $1,000. You don't want to have a balance above $100.

Each card you carry does not have to have a balance report. So, you can select one or two cards that you'll use on a regular basis, and you want to keep the balances low and pay on time.

The third tip is to keep older accounts open. The age of your credit history makes up 15% of your scores. So, keep accounts open and let them gain age or history, which can improve your scores over time. The only exception I will say is if you're carrying subprime accounts and subprime accounts would be your credit cards that are like store credit cards like Victoria's Secret or the Children's Place.

Those are subprime. You want to let those go, especially after you've restored your credit and you start making improvements to your score, you can let those accounts go.

Fourth tip, which is only add new accounts sparingly because new credit makes up 10% of your score and too many of them over a short period can decrease your credit score.

Now if you're rebuilding your credit or you don't have any credit, so you're trying to build up that credit, adding a new positive credit is very necessary. That is the only way that you're going to get your score improved. But you do not want to add too many of these because then you go into the inquiries on your report, which is not a good idea. So, you can add maybe one or two credit cards if you are rebuilding your credit.

The fifth tip is to have more than one form of credit. You want to have a strong credit profile, both credit cards and installment types reporting on your credit report. Credit mix is 10% of your score and it factors into your scores less than any other area that we discussed when you're rebuilding. Having that mixture is essential.

The sixth tip is to create a spending plan. I don't like to call it a budget because I'm not on the budget. I use a spending plan, and this will help you determine where your money is going each month.

My seventh tip is to use technology to help you keep track of your bills. I know a lot of people may not like this but set up automatic payments on your bills and so that the bills are coming out automatically on a regular basis and on time. This will help you to not forget any bills and you can avoid those negative, derogatory late payments. So, setting up automatic payments is huge in keeping up with paying your bills on time.

My final tip is to monitor your credit on a regular basis. This is so important if you are serious about restoring your credit and improving your credit score so that you can meet your goals.

NOTES

CHAPTER TWENTY
DON'T GET SCAMMED

I want to talk about two things here; CPNs and buying Tradelines. A Credit Privacy Number (CPN) is a 9-digit identification number that is sometimes marketed as a way to protect your credit identity and improve your credit score. However, the use of a CPN is not recommended and can lead to legal and financial problems.

CPNs are often marketed as a way to establish a new credit history, but in reality, using a CPN is illegal. It is considered a form of identity theft and can result in criminal charges and legal penalties. Additionally, using a CPN to apply for credit can result in the denial of credit and the creation of a negative mark on your credit report.

In contrast, CPNs are not issued by the government and are not recognized by credit reporting agencies as legitimate.

In addition to being illegal, the use of a CPN can also be costly. If a lender discovers that you have used a CPN to apply for credit, they may report the information to the credit reporting agencies, which can result in it being more difficult for you to obtain credit in the future. If you are caught using a CPN, you may also face legal consequences, including fines and even jail time.

A tradeline refers to a line of credit that appears on your credit report, reflecting your history of borrowing and repaying debts. Essentially, this is just like piggybacking that I talked about in the chapter on Establishing New Credit. The difference here is that you are purchasing a tradeline from someone you don't know. There are some short-term benefits to purchasing a positive tradeline. For a period, you will have that positive tradeline reporting on your credit report.

I want to caution you; you don't know who holds this account. They could remove you from the account as an authorized user at any time. If you are removed, that account history will also be removed from your credit report. This could be a waste of time and money. Also, this is not a guarantee that your credit score will improve. You need to consider your own credit when you are thinking about purchasing a tradeline. If you have a lot of negative accounts on your own credit report, purchasing a tradeline may not help at all.

I insist, please just stay away from CPNs and purchasing tradelines. Work on repairing your own credit. You will get to where you want to be in time.

NOTES

CHAPTER TWENTY-ONE
15/3 CREDIT CARD PAYMENT HACK

The 15/3 credit card hack involves making two credit card payments per month. You will make one payment 15 days before your statement date and then you will make a second payment three days before the statement date.

The statement date is the last day of the credit card's billing period. This is normally when you would receive your billing statement that shows how much you owe and when you owe it. Your billing period is normally about 30 days. Now it's important to note that your statement date is different from your payment date. Your payment date is when you must make your minimum payment. You can find out your statement date by calling the credit card company.

So, let's talk about how the 15/3 hack works:

Say you have a credit card that has a limit of $2,000 and the current billing period is 30 days from May 15th to June 15th. On May 30th, 15 days before the statement date, your balance is $1,000. You make a payment of $750. Your balance is now $250. Over the next 12 days, you spend $500, so your balance is now $750. Three days before your statement date, you make a payment of $750. Say over the next three days, you spend $200. The $200 is what would be reported to the credit bureaus and on your statement. This is a 10% utilization on this particular card.

I recommend if you want to increase your credit score and do it fast, many recommend utilization of 30%. However, having a 10% utilization will increase your score faster. Remember that credit utilization is 30% of your FICO credit score. Having a high credit card utilization each month tells lenders that you max out your cards every month and can suggest that you are more likely to overspend or miss payments.

This is a great way to increase your score fast but don't get caught up on this. If you can't keep up with this, your priority should be making sure you make your payments on time.

NOTES

CHAPTER TWENTY-TWO
WHAT IS DEBT TO INCOME RATIO (DTI) AND WHY SHOULD YOU CARE?

Debt to income ratio is your total monthly debt payment divided by your gross monthly income. This is your wages before taxes and any other deductions are taken out.

So how do you calculate debt to income ratio?

Step one: Add up all your monthly bills. This includes your rent/mortgage, car loans, student loans, medical bills, credit card payments, and personal loans if you have them. You'll also want to include recurring payments like child support and alimony, even though these are technically not considered debt. To get a good picture of what your debt-to-income ratio, you want to include those things.

You don't need to factor in your common living expenses like utilities and food or any paycheck deductions.

Step two: Divide that number by your gross monthly income. Remember, that's the number before taxes are taken out.

Step three: Multiply the number by 100 to get a percentage, and that is going to be your debt-to-income (DTI) ratio.

Let's look at an example. David pays $600 a month in monthly debt payments for student loans and a car payment, plus he pays $1,000 a month for his mortgage before taxes. David brings home $5,000 a month to calculate his DTI. He adds up his monthly debt and mortgage payments. That's $1,600. Remember, he paid $600 in student loans and car payments and another $1,000 in mortgage payment. So, $1,600 divided by $5,000 ($5,000 his gross monthly income) and he gets 0.32. Then he wants to multiply that by 100 to get a percentage. David's debt to income ratio is 32%.

A DTI of less than 36% is viewed as good, and lenders think that you can manage your current debt and you can handle taking on additional debt.

With a DTI between 36% and 43%, lenders start to get a little nervous that adding another loan payment to your plate might be challenging, especially if an emergency pops up.

A DTI between 43 and 50% causes lenders to look at you as high risk and you may not even be able to get a loan.

DTI over 50% is extremely high-risk. Lenders probably won't lend you anything. If you have a DTI that high, that means over 50% of your monthly income is going towards paying debt. If you have a high DTI, I do not suggest taking on any more debt. You can earn additional income, which will shift the DTI. Or you can pay down your debt.

It's your turn to calculate your DTI.

____ Monthly Bills / ____ Gross Monthly Income

What is your Debt-to-Income Ratio (DTI)

____

NOTES

CHAPTER TWENTY-THREE
FREQUENTLY ASKED QUESTIONS

Can Credit Scores Change A Lot?

- Credit Scores can change every day depending on what you are doing with your credit. If you are applying for credit or paying down debt, your credit score will change.

How Do Lenders Use Credit Scores?

- Lenders use credit scores to evaluate an individual's likelihood of repaying a loan and will typically use a higher credit score as a sign that the individual is more likely to repay the loan on time. This information is also used to determine loan terms and interest rates for borrowers.

Are Credit Bureaus Ran By The Government?

- No, credit bureaus are not government agency. However, the Consumer Protection Bureau, which is a government agency, can assist with enforcing consumer laws.

Can Accounts That I Had Remove Reappear on My Credit Report?

- Yes, they can be reinserted back to your credit report, however according to the

Fair Credit Report Act, the credit bureaus have 5 days to send you a letter letting you know. If the credit bureaus do not send this letter in a timely fashion, you should dispute the account. Check out the template I have provided for a dispute letter.

How Do I Keep My Credit Safe?

- Monitor your credit reports regularly to ensure that all the information is accurate and that there are no unauthorized accounts or transactions.

  Use strong and unique passwords for all your financial accounts and be cautious when clicking on links or providing personal information online.

  Be wary of phishing scams and unsolicited phone calls or emails that ask for personal information or money.

  Keep your credit card and other financial information secure by not sharing it with others, including family or friends.

Why Did My Credit Score Decrease When I

Paid Off An Account?

- Paying off an account, especially a credit card, may lower your overall credit utilization ratio, which is the amount of credit you're using compared to the amount of credit available to you. A lower credit utilization ratio can be seen as a positive factor by credit scoring models, but it may also cause your overall credit mix to change. Don't worry, your score will rebound in a couple of months.

What Is A Good Credit Score?

- As I said before, don't worry so much about your score because they will go up and down. However, a good credit score typically falls in the range of 670 to 739 on the FICO score scale, which is the most widely used credit scoring model. A score in this range is considered "good" and can make it easier to qualify for loans and credit cards with favorable terms and rates. However, a score of 800 or higher is considered "excellent" and can get even better rates.

Can I Get A Loan Or Credit Card With Bad Credit?

- Yes, it is possible to get a loan or credit card with bad credit, but it may be more difficult, and the terms may not be as favorable as they would be for someone with good credit. Some lenders specialize in providing loans or credit cards to people with bad credit, but they may charge higher interest rates and fees.

Why Do I Have So Many Credit Scores?

- You may have multiple credit scores because different credit reporting agencies and lenders use different methods to calculate credit scores, and they may also use different credit reporting data.

How Long Do Collections Stay On Your Credit Report?

- Collections stay on your credit report for at least seven years unless you dispute them.

Why are Credit Karma Scores So Different?

- Credit Karma scores are so different because they use Vantage scores, not the FICO scoring model that is widely used. The VantageScore was created by the three major credit bureaus, Experian, TransUnion, and Equifax. It was created to compete with the FICO scoring model.

Should I Use Experian Boost To Help Increase My Credit Score?

- No, Experian boost really doesn't help. Lenders don't consider those boosted accounts when you apply for credit.

Is it Best To Pay More Than My Credit Card Minimum?

- It is generally best to pay more than the minimum payment on a credit card. The minimum payment is usually only a small percentage of the total balance, and if you only make the minimum payment, it will take much longer to pay off the balance and you will end up paying more in interest charges.

What is Credit Monitoring?

- Credit monitoring is a service that helps individuals track and monitor their credit history and score. It can alert users to potentially fraudulent activity or changes to their credit report, such as new accounts opened in their name or changes to their personal information. This can help individuals detect and address identity theft or errors on their credit reports in a timely manner. Some credit monitoring services also provide credit score tracking and educational resources to help users improve their credit.

Should I Send My Disputes Certified?

- Whether you send certified or not, everyone's dispute should be investigated within the 30–45-day timeframe. Sending certified does not change this. However, when you send letters to credit bureaus, collection agencies, lenders, and creditors, you can send certified with the return receipt requested. This gives you proof that your letter has been sent and received. If you ever need to file a complaint, you will have that proof.

Does Your Credit Score Affect Your Car Insurance?

- Yes, insurance companies look at your credit report before giving you a quote for insurance. The lower your score, the more the company feels that you are a higher risk for filing an insurance claim.

How Long Does Credit Repair Take?

- Credit repair is not an overnight process. Remember this is going to take time. You need to remain consistent and persistent.

How much should my credit score increase?

- If you remain consistent with disputing errors on your credit report and paying off debt you will see a change in your credit score in a short timeframe. However, a significant change will take time.

Should I use a debt management company?

- I do not suggest using debt management companies. Most of these companies require that you make payment on an account for at least three years before they will try to settle your debt. Even with this many times a lender may not negotiate with the company. Debt management companies also suggest that you stop making payment on your accounts, I would never recommend this.

NOTES

CHAPTER TWENTY-FOUR
10 COMMONT CREDIT MISTAKES TO AVIOID

1. Missing Payments: Late payments can negatively impact your credit score and result in late fees and interest charges.

2. Maxing out Credit Cards: Using up all of your available credit can make it harder to pay off your balances and increase your credit utilization ratio, which can negatively impact your credit score.

3. Applying for Too Many Credit Cards: Applying for multiple credit cards at once can lead to multiple hard inquiries on your credit report, which can lower your credit score.

4. Closing Credit Card Accounts: Closing credit card accounts can decrease your available credit and increase your credit utilization ratio, which can negatively impact your credit score.

5. Ignoring Your Credit Report: Failing to regularly review your credit report can lead to errors going unnoticed and potential fraud going undetected.

6. Co-signing for Loans: Co-signing for someone else's loan can put you at risk of being responsible for their debt if they default.

7. Not Using Credit Responsibly: Using credit irresponsibly can lead to overspending, high levels of debt, and difficulty making payments, which can negatively impact your credit score and financial health.

8. Neglecting to Establish Credit: If you're new to credit, it's important to establish a credit history in order to build a credit score. Neglecting to do so can make it difficult to obtain credit in the future.

9. Not Paying Attention to Interest Rates: Failing to pay attention to interest rates can lead to high levels of debt and increased interest charges, which can be difficult to pay off.

10. Ignoring Credit Utilization: Credit utilization refers to the amount of available credit you're using. Using too

much of your available credit can negatively impact your credit score, so it's important to keep your credit utilization ratio low by paying off balances in full or keeping balances low.

NOTES

CHAPTER TWENTY-FIVE
DISPUTE LETTER EXAMPLES

On the next few pages, you will find examples that will give you an idea of the dispute letters that you should be writing.

Sample Inquiry Dispute – Original Creditor

Date:
Company's Name
Address
City, State Zip

Re: Unauthorized credit inquiry

To Whom It May Concern:

While checking my personal credit report, which I acquired from [insert Credit bureau name], I notice an inquiry made by your organization.

Since I have not authorized anyone employed by your organization to make an inquiry, you are not legally entitled to make the inquiry. Therefore, I request that you contact the concerned credit bureau and remove the unauthorized hard inquiry immediately.

I also request that you remove my personal information from your records. Please send me a written confirmation that you have complied with my requests.

If you believe that you possess sufficient documentation that supports your authorization to make the inquiry, please send me a copy to my current address so that I may verify its validity.

Sincerely,
NAME **(DO NOT SIGN)**

Sample Inquiry Dispute – Credit Bureau

Date:
Name
Address
City, State Zip

Credit Bureau's Name
Address
City, State, Zip Code

RE: Credit Inquiry Removal Request

Dear Credit Bureau:

The purpose of this letter is to have several unauthorized credit inquiries removed from my credit report. I have received a copy of my credit report from your bureau on DATE and noticed that there are (# of inquiries) unauthorized inquiries listed. The unauthorized inquiries are listed below, and I have also highlighted them on the enclosed copy of my credit report.

Item One Name of Company

Item Two Name of Financial Institution

Item Three Name of Credit Union

Please remove these unauthorized inquiries and send me a copy of my new, accurate credit report.

Thank you for your timely attention to this matter.

Sincerely,
Name **(DO NOT SIGN)**
(ID/SSN Enclosure)

Sample Goodwill Letter

Date:
Specific Name of Company Rep
Company's address

Re: Account No.

Dear (name of person above)

Last year (or whenever you were late) I became seriously behind on several of my bill; yours included. (explain financial hardship – job loss, divorce, medical problems, etc). While I normally make great effort to honor my debts and fulfill my responsibilities, at the time of the late payments I was simply financially not able to pay my bills.

I have since gotten back on my feet and brought my account up to date with your company.

I am now trying to **(WHATEVER YOU ARE TRYING TO DO WITH YOUR CREDIT EXAMPLE: BUY A HOME);** however, I am having difficulties receiving an affordable rate due to the impact of having a late payment(s) on my credit report. I am hoping that you can give me a second chance and will consider removing this late payment from my credit report as a gesture of goodwill. This kind gesture would sincerely be appreciated and an invaluable gift to my family and me.

I sincerely hope that there is redemption at **(INSERT COMPANY'S NAME)**, and I beg you for such consideration. I thank you again for the time you have spent reading this letter.

Kind Regards
Name
Address
Ph Number

Sample letter to dispute outdated or incorrect personal information

Date:

Name:
Address:
DOB:
SSN:

Dear Credit Bureau,

Upon reviewing the personal information section of my credit report, I noticed that there were several outdated and/or incorrect personal information being reported.
Please see that the following personal information is removed from my credit report.
I have listed the information below:

REMOVE THE FOLLOWING NAMES:

REMOVE THE FOLLOWING ADDRESSES:
REMOVE THE FOLLOWING PHONE NUMBERS:

REMOVE THE FOLLOWING

EMPLOYERS:

Please send me and updated copy of my credit report once this information has been removed.

Sincerely,
NAME **(DO NOT SIGN)**
(ID/SSN ENCLOSURE)

Sample initial dispute

Date:

Name:
Address:
DOB:
SSN:

Dear Credit Bureau,

Upon looking at my credit report, I noticed several accounts on my credit report that is reporting inaccurate. Please see to it that the following accounts are removed from my credit report. I have listed the accounts below:

ACCOUNT NAME:
ACCOUNT NUMBER:

ACCOUNT NAME:
ACCOUNT NUMBER:

Please see to it that these accounts are removed from credit report and send me an updated copy of my credit report once this information has been removed.

Sincerely,
NAME **(DO NOT SIGN)**
(ID/SSN ENCLOSURE)

Sample Decline to do business with collection agency

Date:

Name:
Address:

(DO NOT ENCLOSE DATE OF BIRTH OR SOCIAL SECURITY NUMBER WITH DEBT COLLECTORS)

Name of Collection Agency:
Address:

Dear Collection Agency,

I am writing to decline your business. If you feel the need to force me to do business with you then provide written documentation that makes me obligated to do so (written agreement or contract between us.) If you can't provide that than cease and desist and return this account to whomever asked you to invite me to pay whatever it is you are trying to collect.

Sincerely,
NAME **(DO NOT SIGN)**

NOTES

CHAPTER TWENTY-SIX
CONCLUSION

I want to be the first one to congratulate you. If you have done all the things in this guide, you are on your way to living a better life, not just for yourself but for your family. While it may take some time to see significant changes to your credit score, they will increase. Be patient, be persistent, pay your bills on time, and you will get there. Having good credit feels so good; trust me, I know.

Credit is significant in everyone's life and understanding credit and how it works is the first step to becoming financially free. With good credit, you can leverage it to live the life that you want to live. Good credit can open doors to a wide range of opportunities.

The opportunities are unlimited. The future of credit is likely to involve greater use of technology, such as artificial intelligence, to assess creditworthiness and make lending decisions. This could lead to faster and more efficient credit processing, as well as the ability to reach a wider range of borrowers. Additionally, there may be an increased focus on financial inclusion, with more efforts being made to provide credit access to underserved populations. Another trend could be the use of alternative forms of data, such as social media activity or online behavior, to assess creditworthiness. I want you to be a part of the future of credit. So don't procrastinate.

ABOUT THE AUTHOR

Kiwanis Rucker is on a mission to encourage people not just to live better lives but to leave a legacy while doing so. Known as the credit advisor that you need in your life, she is skilled at helping people leverage their credit to live the life that they deserve. It doesn't matter if she is dropping gems on her credit podcast, social media, or live events; Kiwanis motivates people to want to have a healthy financial life. She understands that her assignment is to help her community tap into their credit to help narrow the wealth gap.

After spending her late 20s and early 30s being denied credit and not really understanding credit, Kiwanis took it upon herself to research everything that she could about credit. Kiwanis was able to increase her credit score by over 100 points within one year. Rucker knew that in her community, there were others just like her that lacked the understanding of credit and how to use it.

As the CEO and Founder of KMJ Financial Services, LLC, Rucker specializes in credit education and tax preparation. She believes through good credit and tax planning; we can begin to close the wealth gap within her community. KMJ Financial Services, LLC offers proven strategies in credit education and tax planning. Her firm's unique approach to good credit and tax planning gives her clients the confidence they need to live better. She believes that there is no shortage of gurus and experts in the credit repair industry. However, what makes her firm different is that if she hasn't tested it, she will not teach it or recommend it to her clients. She practices what she preaches. She is not afraid to share the things that do not work as well as those things that do work. Kiwanis' desire is that her community learn from her mistakes so that they can sidestep any hurdles on their way to excellent credit.

A reliable and transparent leader, conferences such as the Woman 2 Woman and Meeting of the Minds have tapped into Rucker to serve as host. Her community often remarks on how knowledgeable she is about credit and taxes and how she makes these complex topics relevant.

Rucker is also the host of the Credit Refresh podcast, where you can find her, every week giving credit and tax tips that you can use. In her free time, she enjoys relaxing and spending time with her family.

Work With Me

Check Out My **Podcasts**

Check Out My **YouTube**

Printed by Libri Plureos GmbH in Hamburg,
Germany